TAI

MW01611552

1

2

3   25

4   26

5   27

6   28

7   29

8   30

9   31

10   32

11   33

12   34

13   35

14   36

15   37

16   38

17   39

18   40

19   41

20   42

21   43

22   44

I

45

46

47

48

49

50

51

52

53

54

55

56

57

58

59

60

61

62

63

64

65

66

II

67

68

69

70

71

72

73

74

75

76

77

78

79

80

81

82

83

84

85

86

87

88

89 .... 111 ....

90 .... 112 ....

91 .... 113 ....

92 .... 114 ....

93 .... 115 ....

94 .... 116 ....

95 .... 117 ....

96 .... 118 ....

97 .... 119 ....

98 .... 120 ....

99 .... 121 ....

100 .... 122 ....

101 .... 123 ....

102 .... 124 ....

103 .... 125 ....

104 .... 126 ....

105 .... 127 ....

106 .... 128 ....

107 .... 129 ....

108 .... 130 ....

109 .... 131 ....

110 .... 132 ....

133 ....

134 ....

135 ....

136 ....

137 ....

138 ....

139 ....

140 ....

141 ....

142 ....

143 ....

144 ....

145 ....

146 ....

147 ....

148 ....

149 ....

150 ....

151 ....

152 ....

153 ....

154 ....

155 ....

156 ....

157 ....

158 ....

159 ....

160 ....

161 ....

162 ....

163 ....

164 ....

165 ....

166 ....

167 ....

168 ....

169 ....

170 ....

171 ....

172 ....

173 ....

174 ....

175 ....

176 ....

177

178

179

180

181

182

183

184

185

186

187

188

189

190

191

192

193

194

195

196

197

198

199

200

201

202

203

204

205

206

207

208

209

210

211

212

213

214

215

216

217

218

219

220

Site / Account Name:

Example Account

Website: www.examplesite.com

User Name: johndoe

eMail: john@doe.com

Membership / Rewards #:
12345678910

Password: ~~0987654321~~ Date: ~~01/01/2010~~

Password: ~~newpassword~~ Date: ~~01/01/2015~~

Password: Strong@password2 Date: 01/01/2019

Password: Date:

Password: Date:

Password: Date:

Pin#: 1234

Secret Word: winning

Pass-phrase: welcome home

Phone# (associated with account):
949-123-4567

Address: 1234 Main St.
Somewhere, CA
92340

Notes:

Banking website for
my retirement.

Site / Account Name:

Website:

User Name:

eMail:

Membership / Rewards #:

Password: Date:

Password: Date:

Password: Date:

Password: Date:

Password: Date:

Password: Date:

Pin#:   Notes:

Secret Word:

Pass-phrase:

Phone# (associated with account):

Address:

Site / Account Name:

Website:

User Name:

eMail:

Membership / Rewards #:

Password: Date:

Password: Date:

Password: Date:

Password: Date:

Password: Date:

Password: Date:

Pin#:   Notes:

Secret Word:

Pass-phrase:

Phone# (associated with account):

Address:

Site / Account Name:

Website:

User Name:

eMail:

Membership / Rewards #:

Password: Date:

Password: Date:

Password: Date:

Password: Date:

Password: Date:

Password: Date:

Pin#:   Notes:

Secret Word:

Pass-phrase:

Phone# (associated with account):

Address:

Site / Account Name:

Website:

User Name:

eMail:

Membership / Rewards #:

Password: Date:

Password: Date:

Password: Date:

Password: Date:

Password: Date:

Password: Date:

Pin#:   Notes:

Secret Word:

Pass-phrase:

Phone# (associated with account):

Address:

4

Site / Account Name:

Website:

User Name:

eMail:

Membership / Rewards #:

Password: Date:

Password: Date:

Password: Date:

Password: Date:

Password: Date:

Password: Date:

Pin#:   Notes:

Secret Word:

Pass-phrase:

Phone# (associated with account):

Address:

Site / Account Name:

Website:

User Name:

eMail:

Membership / Rewards #:

Password: Date:

Password: Date:

Password: Date:

Password: Date:

Password: Date:

Password: Date:

Pin#:   Notes:

Secret Word:

Pass-phrase:

Phone# (associated with account):

Address:

Site / Account Name:

Website:

User Name:

eMail:

Membership / Rewards #:

Password: _____ Date:

Password: _____ Date:

Password: _____ Date:

Password: _____ Date:

Password: _____ Date:

Password: _____ Date:

Pin#: _____ Notes:

Secret Word:

Pass-phrase:

Phone# (associated with account):

Address:

Site / Account Name:

Website:

User Name:

eMail:

Membership / Rewards #:

Password: Date:

Password: Date:

Password: Date:

Password: Date:

Password: Date:

Password: Date:

Pin#: Notes:

Secret Word:

Pass-phrase:

Phone# (associated with account):

Address:

Site / Account Name:

Website:

User Name:

eMail:

Membership / Rewards #:

Password: Date:

Password: Date:

Password: Date:

Password: Date:

Password: Date:

Password: Date:

Pin#:   Notes:

Secret Word:

Pass-phrase:

Phone# (associated with account):

Address:

Site / Account Name:

Website:

User Name:

eMail:

Membership / Rewards #:

Password: Date:

Password: Date:

Password: Date:

Password: Date:

Password: Date:

Password: Date:

Pin#:   Notes:

Secret Word:

Pass-phrase:

Phone# (associated with account):

Address:

Site / Account Name:

Website:

User Name:

eMail:

Membership / Rewards #:

Password: Date:

Password: Date:

Password: Date:

Password: Date:

Password: Date:

Password: Date:

Pin#:   Notes:

Secret Word:

Pass-phrase:

Phone# (associated with account):

Address:

Site / Account Name:

Website:

User Name:

eMail:

Membership / Rewards #:

Password: _____ Date: _____

Password: _____ Date: _____

Password: _____ Date: _____

Password: _____ Date: _____

Password: _____ Date: _____

Password: _____ Date: _____

Pin#: | Notes:

Secret Word:

Pass-phrase:

Phone# (associated with account):

Address:

Site / Account Name:

Website:

User Name:

eMail:

Membership / Rewards #:

Password: Date:

Password: Date:

Password: Date:

Password: Date:

Password: Date:

Password: Date:

Pin#:   Notes:

Secret Word:

Pass-phrase:

Phone# (associated with account):

Address:

13

Site / Account Name:

Website:

User Name:

eMail:

Membership / Rewards #:

Password: Date:

Password: Date:

Password: Date:

Password: Date:

Password: Date:

Password: Date:

Pin#:   Notes:

Secret Word:

Pass-phrase:

Phone# (associated with account):

Address:

Site / Account Name:

Website:

User Name:

eMail:

Membership / Rewards #:

Password: Date:

Password: Date:

Password: Date:

Password: Date:

Password: Date:

Password: Date:

Pin#:   Notes:

Secret Word:

Pass-phrase:

Phone# (associated with account):

Address:

15

Site / Account Name:

Website:

User Name:

eMail:

Membership / Rewards #:

Password: Date:

Password: Date:

Password: Date:

Password: Date:

Password: Date:

Password: Date:

Pin#:   Notes:

Secret Word:

Pass-phrase:

Phone# (associated with account):

Address:

Site / Account Name:

Website:

User Name:

eMail:

Membership / Rewards #:

Password: .... Date: ....

Password: .... Date: ....

Password: .... Date: ....

Password: .... Date: ....

Password: .... Date: ....

Password: .... Date: ....

Pin#:   Notes:

Secret Word:

Pass-phrase:

Phone# (associated with account):

Address:

Site / Account Name:

Website:

User Name:

eMail:

Membership / Rewards #:

Password: Date:

Password: Date:

Password: Date:

Password: Date:

Password: Date:

Password: Date:

Pin#:   Notes:

Secret Word:

Pass-phrase:

Phone# (associated with account):

Address:

Site / Account Name:

Website:

User Name:

eMail:

Membership / Rewards #:

Password: Date:

Password: Date:

Password: Date:

Password: Date:

Password: Date:

Password: Date:

Pin#: Notes:

Secret Word:

Pass-phrase:

Phone# (associated with account):

Address:

Site / Account Name:

Website:

User Name:

eMail:

Membership / Rewards #:

Password: Date:

Password: Date:

Password: Date:

Password: Date:

Password: Date:

Password: Date:

Pin#:   Notes:

Secret Word:

Pass-phrase:

Phone# (associated with account):

Address:

Site / Account Name:

Website:

User Name:

eMail:

Membership / Rewards #:

Password: Date:

Password: Date:

Password: Date:

Password: Date:

Password: Date:

Password: Date:

Pin#:   Notes:

Secret Word:

Pass-phrase:

Phone# (associated with account):

Address:

21

Site / Account Name:

Website:

User Name:

eMail:

Membership / Rewards #:

Password: Date:

Password: Date:

Password: Date:

Password: Date:

Password: Date:

Password: Date:

Pin#:   Notes:

Secret Word:

Pass-phrase:

Phone# (associated with account):

Address:

Site / Account Name:

Website:

User Name:

eMail:

Membership / Rewards #:

Password: Date:

Password: Date:

Password: Date:

Password: Date:

Password: Date:

Password: Date:

Pin#:   Notes:

Secret Word:

Pass-phrase:

Phone# (associated with account):

Address:

Site / Account Name:

Website:

User Name:

eMail:

Membership / Rewards #:

Password: Date:

Password: Date:

Password: Date:

Password: Date:

Password: Date:

Password: Date:

Pin#: Notes:

Secret Word:

Pass-phrase:

Phone# (associated with account):

Address:

Site / Account Name:

Website:

User Name:

eMail:

Membership / Rewards #:

Password: Date:

Password: Date:

Password: Date:

Password: Date:

Password: Date:

Password: Date:

Pin#:   Notes:

Secret Word:

Pass-phrase:

Phone# (associated with account):

Address:

Site / Account Name:

Website:

User Name:

eMail:

Membership / Rewards #:

Password: Date:

Password: Date:

Password: Date:

Password: Date:

Password: Date:

Password: Date:

Pin#:   Notes:

Secret Word:

Pass-phrase:

Phone# (associated with account):

Address:

Site / Account Name:

Website:

User Name:

eMail:

Membership / Rewards #:

Password: _____ Date: _____

Password: _____ Date: _____

Password: _____ Date: _____

Password: _____ Date: _____

Password: _____ Date: _____

Password: _____ Date: _____

Pin#: | Notes:

Secret Word:

Pass-phrase:

Phone# (associated with account):

Address:

Site / Account Name:

_____

Website:

User Name:

eMail:

Membership / Rewards #:

Password: .... Date:

Password: .... Date:

Password: .... Date:

Password: .... Date:

Password: .... Date:

Password: .... Date:

_____

Pin#:   Notes:

Secret Word:

Pass-phrase:

Phone# (associated with account):

Address:

Site / Account Name:

Website:

User Name:

eMail:

Membership / Rewards #:

Password: Date:

Password: Date:

Password: Date:

Password: Date:

Password: Date:

Password: Date:

Pin#:   Notes:

Secret Word:

Pass-phrase:

Phone# (associated with account):

Address:

29

Site / Account Name:

_____

Website:

User Name:

eMail:

Membership / Rewards #:

Password: .... Date:

Password: .... Date:

Password: .... Date:

Password: .... Date:

Password: .... Date:

Password: .... Date:

_____

Pin#: Notes:

Secret Word:

Pass-phrase:

Phone# (associated with account):

Address:

Site / Account Name:

Website:

User Name:

eMail:

Membership / Rewards #:

Password: Date:

Password: Date:

Password: Date:

Password: Date:

Password: Date:

Password: Date:

Pin#:   Notes:

Secret Word:

Pass-phrase:

Phone# (associated with account):

Address:

Site / Account Name:

Website:

User Name:

eMail:

Membership / Rewards #:

Password: .... Date:

Password: .... Date:

Password: .... Date:

Password: .... Date:

Password: .... Date:

Password: .... Date:

Pin#: .... Notes:

Secret Word:

Pass-phrase:

Phone# (associated with account):

Address:

Site / Account Name:

Website:

User Name:

eMail:

Membership / Rewards #:

Password: Date:

Password: Date:

Password: Date:

Password: Date:

Password: Date:

Password: Date:

Pin#:   Notes:

Secret Word:

Pass-phrase:

Phone# (associated with account):

Address:

Site / Account Name:

Website:

User Name:

eMail:

Membership / Rewards #:

Password: .... Date:

Password: .... Date:

Password: .... Date:

Password: .... Date:

Password: .... Date:

Password: .... Date:

Pin#:   Notes:

Secret Word:

Pass-phrase:

Phone# (associated with account):

Address:

Site / Account Name:

Website:

User Name:

eMail:

Membership / Rewards #:

Password: .... Date:

Password: .... Date:

Password: .... Date:

Password: .... Date:

Password: .... Date:

Password: .... Date:

Pin#: .... Notes:

Secret Word:

Pass-phrase:

Phone# (associated with account):

Address:

Site / Account Name:

Website:

User Name:

eMail:

Membership / Rewards #:

Password: Date:

Password: Date:

Password: Date:

Password: Date:

Password: Date:

Password: Date:

Pin#:   Notes:

Secret Word:

Pass-phrase:

Phone# (associated with account):

Address:

Site / Account Name:

Website:

User Name:

eMail:

Membership / Rewards #:

Password: Date:

Password: Date:

Password: Date:

Password: Date:

Password: Date:

Password: Date:

Pin#: Notes:

Secret Word:

Pass-phrase:

Phone# (associated with account):

Address:

Site / Account Name:

Website:

User Name:

eMail:

Membership / Rewards #:

Password: .... Date:

Password: .... Date:

Password: .... Date:

Password: .... Date:

Password: .... Date:

Password: .... Date:

Pin#: .... Notes:

Secret Word:

Pass-phrase:

Phone# (associated with account):

Address:

Site / Account Name:

Website:

User Name:

eMail:

Membership / Rewards #:

Password: Date:

Password: Date:

Password: Date:

Password: Date:

Password: Date:

Password: Date:

Pin#: Notes:

Secret Word:

Pass-phrase:

Phone# (associated with account):

Address:

Site / Account Name:

Website:

User Name:

eMail:

Membership / Rewards #:

Password: Date:

Password: Date:

Password: Date:

Password: Date:

Password: Date:

Password: Date:

Pin#: Notes:

Secret Word:

Pass-phrase:

Phone# (associated with account):

Address:

Site / Account Name:

Website:

User Name:

eMail:

Membership / Rewards #:

Password: Date:

Password: Date:

Password: Date:

Password: Date:

Password: Date:

Password: Date:

Pin#:   Notes:

Secret Word:

Pass-phrase:

Phone# (associated with account):

Address:

Site / Account Name:

Website:

User Name:

eMail:

Membership / Rewards #:

Password: .... Date:

Password: .... Date:

Password: .... Date:

Password: .... Date:

Password: .... Date:

Password: .... Date:

Pin#:

Secret Word:

Pass-phrase:

Phone# (associated with account):

Address:

Notes:

Site / Account Name:

Website:

User Name:

eMail:

Membership / Rewards #:

Password: Date:

Password: Date:

Password: Date:

Password: Date:

Password: Date:

Password: Date:

Pin#:   Notes:

Secret Word:

Pass-phrase:

Phone# (associated with account):

Address:

Site / Account Name:

Website:

User Name:

eMail:

Membership / Rewards #:

Password: .... Date:

Password: .... Date:

Password: .... Date:

Password: .... Date:

Password: .... Date:

Password: .... Date:

Pin#:   Notes:

Secret Word:

Pass-phrase:

Phone# (associated with account):

Address:

Site / Account Name:

Website:

User Name:

eMail:

Membership / Rewards #:

Password: Date:

Password: Date:

Password: Date:

Password: Date:

Password: Date:

Password: Date:

Pin#:   Notes:

Secret Word:

Pass-phrase:

Phone# (associated with account):

Address:

Site / Account Name:

Website:

User Name:

eMail:

Membership / Rewards #:

Password: Date:

Password: Date:

Password: Date:

Password: Date:

Password: Date:

Password: Date:

Pin#:   Notes:

Secret Word:

Pass-phrase:

Phone# (associated with account):

Address:

Site / Account Name:

Website:

User Name:

eMail:

Membership / Rewards #:

Password: Date:

Password: Date:

Password: Date:

Password: Date:

Password: Date:

Password: Date:

Pin#:   Notes:

Secret Word:

Pass-phrase:

Phone# (associated with account):

Address:

Site / Account Name:

Website:

User Name:

eMail:

Membership / Rewards #:

Password: Date:

Password: Date:

Password: Date:

Password: Date:

Password: Date:

Password: Date:

Pin#:   Notes:

Secret Word:

Pass-phrase:

Phone# (associated with account):

Address:

Site / Account Name:

Website:

User Name:

eMail:

Membership / Rewards #:

Password: Date:

Password: Date:

Password: Date:

Password: Date:

Password: Date:

Password: Date:

Pin#: Notes:

Secret Word:

Pass-phrase:

Phone# (associated with account):

Address:

Site / Account Name:

Website:

User Name:

eMail:

Membership / Rewards #:

Password: Date:

Password: Date:

Password: Date:

Password: Date:

Password: Date:

Password: Date:

Pin#:   Notes:

Secret Word:

Pass-phrase:

Phone# (associated with account):

Address:

Site / Account Name:

Website:

User Name:

eMail:

Membership / Rewards #:

Password: Date:

Password: Date:

Password: Date:

Password: Date:

Password: Date:

Password: Date:

Pin#: Notes:

Secret Word:

Pass-phrase:

Phone# (associated with account):

Address:

Site / Account Name:

Website:

User Name:

eMail:

Membership / Rewards #:

Password: Date:

Password: Date:

Password: Date:

Password: Date:

Password: Date:

Password: Date:

Pin#: Notes:

Secret Word:

Pass-phrase:

Phone# (associated with account):

Address:

Site / Account Name:

Website:

User Name:

eMail:

Membership / Rewards #:

Password: Date:

Password: Date:

Password: Date:

Password: Date:

Password: Date:

Password: Date:

Pin#: Notes:

Secret Word:

Pass-phrase:

Phone# (associated with account):

Address:

Site / Account Name:

Website:

User Name:

eMail:

Membership / Rewards #:

Password: .... Date:

Password: .... Date:

Password: .... Date:

Password: .... Date:

Password: .... Date:

Password: .... Date:

Pin#:   Notes:

Secret Word:

Pass-phrase:

Phone# (associated with account):

Address:

54

Site / Account Name:

Website:

User Name:

eMail:

Membership / Rewards #:

Password: Date:

Password: Date:

Password: Date:

Password: Date:

Password: Date:

Password: Date:

Pin#:   Notes:

Secret Word:

Pass-phrase:

Phone# (associated with account):

Address:

Site / Account Name:

Website:

User Name:

eMail:

Membership / Rewards #:

Password: Date:

Password: Date:

Password: Date:

Password: Date:

Password: Date:

Password: Date:

Pin#: Notes:

Secret Word:

Pass-phrase:

Phone# (associated with account):

Address:

Site / Account Name:

Website:

User Name:

eMail:

Membership / Rewards #:

Password: Date:

Password: Date:

Password: Date:

Password: Date:

Password: Date:

Password: Date:

Pin#: Notes:

Secret Word:

Pass-phrase:

Phone# (associated with account):

Address:

Site / Account Name:

Website:

User Name:

eMail:

Membership / Rewards #:

Password: Date:

Password: Date:

Password: Date:

Password: Date:

Password: Date:

Password: Date:

Pin#:   Notes:

Secret Word:

Pass-phrase:

Phone# (associated with account):

Address:

Site / Account Name:

Website:

User Name:

eMail:

Membership / Rewards #:

Password: Date:

Password: Date:

Password: Date:

Password: Date:

Password: Date:

Password: Date:

Pin#:   Notes:

Secret Word:

Pass-phrase:

Phone# (associated with account):

Address:

Site / Account Name:

Website:

User Name:

eMail:

Membership / Rewards #:

Password: Date:

Password: Date:

Password: Date:

Password: Date:

Password: Date:

Password: Date:

Pin#:   Notes:

Secret Word:

Pass-phrase:

Phone# (associated with account):

Address:

Site / Account Name:

Website:

User Name:

eMail:

Membership / Rewards #:

Password: .... Date:

Password: .... Date:

Password: .... Date:

Password: .... Date:

Password: .... Date:

Password: .... Date:

Pin#:   Notes:

Secret Word:

Pass-phrase:

Phone# (associated with account):

Address:

Site / Account Name:

Website:

User Name:

eMail:

Membership / Rewards #:

Password: Date:

Password: Date:

Password: Date:

Password: Date:

Password: Date:

Password: Date:

Pin#:   Notes:

Secret Word:

Pass-phrase:

Phone# (associated with account):

Address:

Site / Account Name:

Website:

User Name:

eMail:

Membership / Rewards #:

Password: .... Date:

Password: .... Date:

Password: .... Date:

Password: .... Date:

Password: .... Date:

Password: .... Date:

Pin#: | Notes:

Secret Word:

Pass-phrase:

Phone# (associated with account):

Address:

Site / Account Name:

Website:

User Name:

eMail:

Membership / Rewards #:

Password: .... Date:

Password: .... Date:

Password: .... Date:

Password: .... Date:

Password: .... Date:

Password: .... Date:

Pin#:   Notes:

Secret Word:

Pass-phrase:

Phone# (associated with account):

Address:

Site / Account Name:

Website:

User Name:

eMail:

Membership / Rewards #:

Password: Date:

Password: Date:

Password: Date:

Password: Date:

Password: Date:

Password: Date:

Pin#:   Notes:

Secret Word:

Pass-phrase:

Phone# (associated with account):

Address:

Site / Account Name:

Website:

User Name:

eMail:

Membership / Rewards #:

Password: Date:

Password: Date:

Password: Date:

Password: Date:

Password: Date:

Password: Date:

Pin#: Notes:

Secret Word:

Pass-phrase:

Phone# (associated with account):

Address:

Site / Account Name:

Website:

User Name:

eMail:

Membership / Rewards #:

Password: Date:

Password: Date:

Password: Date:

Password: Date:

Password: Date:

Password: Date:

Pin#:   Notes:

Secret Word:

Pass-phrase:

Phone# (associated with account):

Address:

Site / Account Name:

Website:

User Name:

eMail:

Membership / Rewards #:

Password: .... Date:

Password: .... Date:

Password: .... Date:

Password: .... Date:

Password: .... Date:

Password: .... Date:

Pin#: Notes:

Secret Word:

Pass-phrase:

Phone# (associated with account):

Address:

Site / Account Name:

Website:

User Name:

eMail:

Membership / Rewards #:

Password: Date:

Password: Date:

Password: Date:

Password: Date:

Password: Date:

Password: Date:

Pin#: Notes:

Secret Word:

Pass-phrase:

Phone# (associated with account):

Address:

Site / Account Name:

Website:

User Name:

eMail:

Membership / Rewards #:

Password: Date:

Password: Date:

Password: Date:

Password: Date:

Password: Date:

Password: Date:

Pin#:   Notes:

Secret Word:

Pass-phrase:

Phone# (associated with account):

Address:

Site / Account Name:

Website:

User Name:

eMail:

Membership / Rewards #:

Password: Date:

Password: Date:

Password: Date:

Password: Date:

Password: Date:

Password: Date:

Pin#: Notes:

Secret Word:

Pass-phrase:

Phone# (associated with account):

Address:

Site / Account Name:

Website:

User Name:

eMail:

Membership / Rewards #:

Password: .... Date:

Password: .... Date:

Password: .... Date:

Password: .... Date:

Password: .... Date:

Password: .... Date:

Pin#: Notes:

Secret Word:

Pass-phrase:

Phone# (associated with account):

Address:

Site / Account Name:

Website:

User Name:

eMail:

Membership / Rewards #:

Password: Date:

Password: Date:

Password: Date:

Password: Date:

Password: Date:

Password: Date:

Pin#:   Notes:

Secret Word:

Pass-phrase:

Phone# (associated with account):

Address:

Site / Account Name:

Website:

User Name:

eMail:

Membership / Rewards #:

Password: Date:

Password: Date:

Password: Date:

Password: Date:

Password: Date:

Password: Date:

Pin#:   Notes:

Secret Word:

Pass-phrase:

Phone# (associated with account):

Address:

Site / Account Name:

Website:

User Name:

eMail:

Membership / Rewards #:

Password: Date:

Password: Date:

Password: Date:

Password: Date:

Password: Date:

Password: Date:

Pin#:   Notes:

Secret Word:

Pass-phrase:

Phone# (associated with account):

Address:

Site / Account Name:

Website:

User Name:

eMail:

Membership / Rewards #:

Password: Date:

Password: Date:

Password: Date:

Password: Date:

Password: Date:

Password: Date:

Pin#: Notes:

Secret Word:

Pass-phrase:

Phone# (associated with account):

Address:

Site / Account Name:

Website:

User Name:

eMail:

Membership / Rewards #:

Password: Date:

Password: Date:

Password: Date:

Password: Date:

Password: Date:

Password: Date:

Pin#:   Notes:

Secret Word:

Pass-phrase:

Phone# (associated with account):

Address:

Site / Account Name:

Website:

User Name:

eMail:

Membership / Rewards #:

Password: Date:

Password: Date:

Password: Date:

Password: Date:

Password: Date:

Password: Date:

Pin#: Notes:

Secret Word:

Pass-phrase:

Phone# (associated with account):

Address:

Site / Account Name:

Website:

User Name:

eMail:

Membership / Rewards #:

Password: Date:

Password: Date:

Password: Date:

Password: Date:

Password: Date:

Password: Date:

Pin#:   Notes:

Secret Word:

Pass-phrase:

Phone# (associated with account):

Address:

Site / Account Name:

Website:

User Name:

eMail:

Membership / Rewards #:

Password: Date:

Password: Date:

Password: Date:

Password: Date:

Password: Date:

Password: Date:

Pin#:   Notes:

Secret Word:

Pass-phrase:

Phone# (associated with account):

Address:

Site / Account Name:

Website:

User Name:

eMail:

Membership / Rewards #:

Password: Date:

Password: Date:

Password: Date:

Password: Date:

Password: Date:

Password: Date:

Pin#:   Notes:

Secret Word:

Pass-phrase:

Phone# (associated with account):

Address:

Site / Account Name:

Website:

User Name:

eMail:

Membership / Rewards #:

Password: Date:

Password: Date:

Password: Date:

Password: Date:

Password: Date:

Password: Date:

Pin#: Notes:

Secret Word:

Pass-phrase:

Phone# (associated with account):

Address:

Site / Account Name:

Website:

User Name:

eMail:

Membership / Rewards #:

Password: .... Date:

Password: .... Date:

Password: .... Date:

Password: .... Date:

Password: .... Date:

Password: .... Date:

Pin#:   Notes:

Secret Word:

Pass-phrase:

Phone# (associated with account):

Address:

Site / Account Name:

Website:

User Name:

eMail:

Membership / Rewards #:

Password: .... Date:

Password: .... Date:

Password: .... Date:

Password: .... Date:

Password: .... Date:

Password: .... Date:

Pin#:   Notes:

Secret Word:

Pass-phrase:

Phone# (associated with account):

Address:

Site / Account Name:

Website:

User Name:

eMail:

Membership / Rewards #:

Password: Date:

Password: Date:

Password: Date:

Password: Date:

Password: Date:

Password: Date:

Pin#:   Notes:

Secret Word:

Pass-phrase:

Phone# (associated with account):

Address:

Site / Account Name:

Website:

User Name:

eMail:

Membership / Rewards #:

Password: Date:

Password: Date:

Password: Date:

Password: Date:

Password: Date:

Password: Date:

Pin#:   Notes:

Secret Word:

Pass-phrase:

Phone# (associated with account):

Address:

Site / Account Name:

Website:

User Name:

eMail:

Membership / Rewards #:

Password: Date:

Password: Date:

Password: Date:

Password: Date:

Password: Date:

Password: Date:

Pin#:   Notes:

Secret Word:

Pass-phrase:

Phone# (associated with account):

Address:

Site / Account Name:

Website:

User Name:

eMail:

Membership / Rewards #:

Password: Date:

Password: Date:

Password: Date:

Password: Date:

Password: Date:

Password: Date:

Pin#: Notes:

Secret Word:

Pass-phrase:

Phone# (associated with account):

Address:

Site / Account Name:

Website:

User Name:

eMail:

Membership / Rewards #:

Password: Date:

Password: Date:

Password: Date:

Password: Date:

Password: Date:

Password: Date:

Pin#:   Notes:

Secret Word:

Pass-phrase:

Phone# (associated with account):

Address:

Site / Account Name:

Website:

User Name:

eMail:

Membership / Rewards #:

Password: .... Date:

Password: .... Date:

Password: .... Date:

Password: .... Date:

Password: .... Date:

Password: .... Date:

Pin#:   Notes:

Secret Word:

Pass-phrase:

Phone# (associated with account):

Address:

Site / Account Name:

Website:

User Name:

eMail:

Membership / Rewards #:

Password: Date:

Password: Date:

Password: Date:

Password: Date:

Password: Date:

Password: Date:

Pin#:   Notes:

Secret Word:

Pass-phrase:

Phone# (associated with account):

Address:

Site / Account Name:

Website:

User Name:

eMail:

Membership / Rewards #:

Password: Date:

Password: Date:

Password: Date:

Password: Date:

Password: Date:

Password: Date:

Pin#: Notes:

Secret Word:

Pass-phrase:

Phone# (associated with account):

Address:

Site / Account Name:

Website:

User Name:

eMail:

Membership / Rewards #:

Password: Date:

Password: Date:

Password: Date:

Password: Date:

Password: Date:

Password: Date:

Pin#: Notes:

Secret Word:

Pass-phrase:

Phone# (associated with account):

Address:

Site / Account Name:

Website:

User Name:

eMail:

Membership / Rewards #:

Password: .... Date:

Password: .... Date:

Password: .... Date:

Password: .... Date:

Password: .... Date:

Password: .... Date:

Pin#: Notes:

Secret Word:

Pass-phrase:

Phone# (associated with account):

Address:

Site / Account Name:

Website:

User Name:

eMail:

Membership / Rewards #:

Password: Date:

Password: Date:

Password: Date:

Password: Date:

Password: Date:

Password: Date:

Pin#:   Notes:

Secret Word:

Pass-phrase:

Phone# (associated with account):

Address:

Site / Account Name:

Website:

User Name:

eMail:

Membership / Rewards #:

Password: Date:

Password: Date:

Password: Date:

Password: Date:

Password: Date:

Password: Date:

Pin#: Notes:

Secret Word:

Pass-phrase:

Phone# (associated with account):

Address:

Site / Account Name:

Website:

User Name:

eMail:

Membership / Rewards #:

Password: Date:

Password: Date:

Password: Date:

Password: Date:

Password: Date:

Password: Date:

Pin#:   Notes:

Secret Word:

Pass-phrase:

Phone# (associated with account):

Address:

Site / Account Name:

Website:

User Name:

eMail:

Membership / Rewards #:

Password: Date:

Password: Date:

Password: Date:

Password: Date:

Password: Date:

Password: Date:

Pin#: Notes:

Secret Word:

Pass-phrase:

Phone# (associated with account):

Address:

Site / Account Name:

Website:

User Name:

eMail:

Membership / Rewards #:

Password: Date:

Password: Date:

Password: Date:

Password: Date:

Password: Date:

Password: Date:

Pin#:   Notes:

Secret Word:

Pass-phrase:

Phone# (associated with account):

Address:

Site / Account Name:

Website:

User Name:

eMail:

Membership / Rewards #:

Password: Date:

Password: Date:

Password: Date:

Password: Date:

Password: Date:

Password: Date:

Pin#:   Notes:

Secret Word:

Pass-phrase:

Phone# (associated with account):

Address:

Site / Account Name:

Website:

User Name:

eMail:

Membership / Rewards #:

Password: Date:

Password: Date:

Password: Date:

Password: Date:

Password: Date:

Password: Date:

Pin#: Notes:

Secret Word:

Pass-phrase:

Phone# (associated with account):

Address:

Site / Account Name:

Website:

User Name:

eMail:

Membership / Rewards #:

Password: Date:

Password: Date:

Password: Date:

Password: Date:

Password: Date:

Password: Date:

Pin#:   Notes:

Secret Word:

Pass-phrase:

Phone# (associated with account):

Address:

Site / Account Name:

Website:

User Name:

eMail:

Membership / Rewards #:

Password: Date:

Password: Date:

Password: Date:

Password: Date:

Password: Date:

Password: Date:

Pin#:   Notes:

Secret Word:

Pass-phrase:

Phone# (associated with account):

Address:

Site / Account Name:

Website:

User Name:

eMail:

Membership / Rewards #:

Password: .... Date:

Password: .... Date:

Password: .... Date:

Password: .... Date:

Password: .... Date:

Password: .... Date:

Pin#:

Secret Word:

Pass-phrase:

Phone# (associated with account):

Address:

Notes:

Site / Account Name:

Website:

User Name:

eMail:

Membership / Rewards #:

Password: Date:

Password: Date:

Password: Date:

Password: Date:

Password: Date:

Password: Date:

Pin#:   Notes:

Secret Word:

Pass-phrase:

Phone# (associated with account):

Address:

Site / Account Name:

Website:

User Name:

eMail:

Membership / Rewards #:

Password: Date:

Password: Date:

Password: Date:

Password: Date:

Password: Date:

Password: Date:

Pin#: Notes:

Secret Word:

Pass-phrase:

Phone# (associated with account):

Address:

Site / Account Name:

Website:

User Name:

eMail:

Membership / Rewards #:

Password: Date:

Password: Date:

Password: Date:

Password: Date:

Password: Date:

Password: Date:

Pin#:   Notes:

Secret Word:

Pass-phrase:

Phone# (associated with account):

Address:

Site / Account Name:

Website:

User Name:

eMail:

Membership / Rewards #:

Password: Date:

Password: Date:

Password: Date:

Password: Date:

Password: Date:

Password: Date:

Pin#:   Notes:

Secret Word:

Pass-phrase:

Phone# (associated with account):

Address:

Site / Account Name:

Website:

User Name:

eMail:

Membership / Rewards #:

Password: Date:

Password: Date:

Password: Date:

Password: Date:

Password: Date:

Password: Date:

Pin#: Notes:

Secret Word:

Pass-phrase:

Phone# (associated with account):

Address:

Site / Account Name:

Website:

User Name:

eMail:

Membership / Rewards #:

Password: Date:

Password: Date:

Password: Date:

Password: Date:

Password: Date:

Password: Date:

Pin#: Notes:

Secret Word:

Pass-phrase:

Phone# (associated with account):

Address:

Site / Account Name:

Website:

User Name:

eMail:

Membership / Rewards #:

Password: Date:

Password: Date:

Password: Date:

Password: Date:

Password: Date:

Password: Date:

Pin#:   Notes:

Secret Word:

Pass-phrase:

Phone# (associated with account):

Address:

Site / Account Name:

Website:

User Name:

eMail:

Membership / Rewards #:

Password: _____ Date:

Password: _____ Date:

Password: _____ Date:

Password: _____ Date:

Password: _____ Date:

Password: _____ Date:

Pin#:   Notes:

Secret Word:

Pass-phrase:

Phone# (associated with account):

Address:

Site / Account Name:

Website:

User Name:

eMail:

Membership / Rewards #:

Password: Date:

Password: Date:

Password: Date:

Password: Date:

Password: Date:

Password: Date:

Pin#:   Notes:

Secret Word:

Pass-phrase:

Phone# (associated with account):

Address:

Site / Account Name:

Website:

User Name:

eMail:

Membership / Rewards #:

Password: Date:

Password: Date:

Password: Date:

Password: Date:

Password: Date:

Password: Date:

Pin#:   Notes:

Secret Word:

Pass-phrase:

Phone# (associated with account):

Address:

Site / Account Name:

Website:

User Name:

eMail:

Membership / Rewards #:

Password: Date:

Password: Date:

Password: Date:

Password: Date:

Password: Date:

Password: Date:

Pin#:   Notes:

Secret Word:

Pass-phrase:

Phone# (associated with account):

Address:

Site / Account Name:

Website:

User Name:

eMail:

Membership / Rewards #:

Password: Date:

Password: Date:

Password: Date:

Password: Date:

Password: Date:

Password: Date:

Pin#: Notes:

Secret Word:

Pass-phrase:

Phone# (associated with account):

Address:

Site / Account Name:

Website:

User Name:

eMail:

Membership / Rewards #:

Password: Date:

Password: Date:

Password: Date:

Password: Date:

Password: Date:

Password: Date:

Pin#:   Notes:

Secret Word:

Pass-phrase:

Phone# (associated with account):

Address:

Site / Account Name:

Website:

User Name:

eMail:

Membership / Rewards #:

Password: Date:

Password: Date:

Password: Date:

Password: Date:

Password: Date:

Password: Date:

Pin#:   Notes:

Secret Word:

Pass-phrase:

Phone# (associated with account):

Address:

Site / Account Name:

Website:

User Name:

eMail:

Membership / Rewards #:

Password: Date:

Password: Date:

Password: Date:

Password: Date:

Password: Date:

Password: Date:

Pin#:   Notes:

Secret Word:

Pass-phrase:

Phone# (associated with account):

Address:

Site / Account Name:

Website:

User Name:

eMail:

Membership / Rewards #:

Password: Date:

Password: Date:

Password: Date:

Password: Date:

Password: Date:

Password: Date:

Pin#:   Notes:

Secret Word:

Pass-phrase:

Phone# (associated with account):

Address:

Site / Account Name:

Website:

User Name:

eMail:

Membership / Rewards #:

Password: _____ Date:

Password: _____ Date:

Password: _____ Date:

Password: _____ Date:

Password: _____ Date:

Password: _____ Date:

Pin#: | Notes:

Secret Word:

Pass-phrase:

Phone# (associated with account):

Address:

Site / Account Name:

Website:

User Name:

eMail:

Membership / Rewards #:

Password: Date:

Password: Date:

Password: Date:

Password: Date:

Password: Date:

Password: Date:

Pin#: Notes:

Secret Word:

Pass-phrase:

Phone# (associated with account):

Address:

Site / Account Name:

Website:

User Name:

eMail:

Membership / Rewards #:

Password: Date:

Password: Date:

Password: Date:

Password: Date:

Password: Date:

Password: Date:

Pin#:   Notes:

Secret Word:

Pass-phrase:

Phone# (associated with account):

Address:

Site / Account Name:

Website:

User Name:

eMail:

Membership / Rewards #:

Password: _____ Date:

Password: _____ Date:

Password: _____ Date:

Password: _____ Date:

Password: _____ Date:

Password: _____ Date:

Pin#:   Notes:

Secret Word:

Pass-phrase:

Phone# (associated with account):

Address:

Site / Account Name:

Website:

User Name:

eMail:

Membership / Rewards #:

Password: Date:

Password: Date:

Password: Date:

Password: Date:

Password: Date:

Password: Date:

Pin#: Notes:

Secret Word:

Pass-phrase:

Phone# (associated with account):

Address:

Site / Account Name:

Website:

User Name:

eMail:

Membership / Rewards #:

Password: _____ Date: _____

Password: _____ Date: _____

Password: _____ Date: _____

Password: _____ Date: _____

Password: _____ Date: _____

Password: _____ Date: _____

Pin#: Notes:

Secret Word:

Pass-phrase:

Phone# (associated with account):

Address:

Site / Account Name:

Website:

User Name:

eMail:

Membership / Rewards #:

Password: Date:

Password: Date:

Password: Date:

Password: Date:

Password: Date:

Password: Date:

Pin#: Notes:

Secret Word:

Pass-phrase:

Phone# (associated with account):

Address:

Site / Account Name:

Website:

User Name:

eMail:

Membership / Rewards #:

Password: Date:

Password: Date:

Password: Date:

Password: Date:

Password: Date:

Password: Date:

Pin#: Notes:

Secret Word:

Pass-phrase:

Phone# (associated with account):

Address:

Site / Account Name:

Website:

User Name:

eMail:

Membership / Rewards #:

Password: Date:

Password: Date:

Password: Date:

Password: Date:

Password: Date:

Password: Date:

Pin#: Notes:

Secret Word:

Pass-phrase:

Phone# (associated with account):

Address:

Site / Account Name:

Website:

User Name:

eMail:

Membership / Rewards #:

Password: Date:

Password: Date:

Password: Date:

Password: Date:

Password: Date:

Password: Date:

Pin#:   Notes:

Secret Word:

Pass-phrase:

Phone# (associated with account):

Address:

Site / Account Name:

Website:

User Name:

eMail:

Membership / Rewards #:

Password: .... Date:

Password: .... Date:

Password: .... Date:

Password: .... Date:

Password: .... Date:

Password: .... Date:

Pin#: .... Notes:

Secret Word:

Pass-phrase:

Phone# (associated with account):

Address:

Site / Account Name:

Website:

User Name:

eMail:

Membership / Rewards #:

Password: Date:

Password: Date:

Password: Date:

Password: Date:

Password: Date:

Password: Date:

Pin#: Notes:

Secret Word:

Pass-phrase:

Phone# (associated with account):

Address:

Site / Account Name:

Website:

User Name:

eMail:

Membership / Rewards #:

Password: Date:

Password: Date:

Password: Date:

Password: Date:

Password: Date:

Password: Date:

Pin#:   Notes:

Secret Word:

Pass-phrase:

Phone# (associated with account):

Address:

Site / Account Name:

Website:

User Name:

eMail:

Membership / Rewards #:

Password: Date:

Password: Date:

Password: Date:

Password: Date:

Password: Date:

Password: Date:

Pin#:   Notes:

Secret Word:

Pass-phrase:

Phone# (associated with account):

Address:

Site / Account Name:

Website:

User Name:

eMail:

Membership / Rewards #:

Password: Date:

Password: Date:

Password: Date:

Password: Date:

Password: Date:

Password: Date:

Pin#:   Notes:

Secret Word:

Pass-phrase:

Phone# (associated with account):

Address:

Site / Account Name:

Website:

User Name:

eMail:

Membership / Rewards #:

Password: Date:

Password: Date:

Password: Date:

Password: Date:

Password: Date:

Password: Date:

Pin#:   Notes:

Secret Word:

Pass-phrase:

Phone# (associated with account):

Address:

Site / Account Name:

Website:

User Name:

eMail:

Membership / Rewards #:

Password: Date:

Password: Date:

Password: Date:

Password: Date:

Password: Date:

Password: Date:

Pin#:   Notes:

Secret Word:

Pass-phrase:

Phone# (associated with account):

Address:

Site / Account Name:

Website:

User Name:

eMail:

Membership / Rewards #:

Password: Date:

Password: Date:

Password: Date:

Password: Date:

Password: Date:

Password: Date:

Pin#:   Notes:

Secret Word:

Pass-phrase:

Phone# (associated with account):

Address:

Site / Account Name:

Website:

User Name:

eMail:

Membership / Rewards #:

Password: .... Date:

Password: .... Date:

Password: .... Date:

Password: .... Date:

Password: .... Date:

Password: .... Date:

Pin#: .... Notes:

Secret Word:

Pass-phrase:

Phone# (associated with account):

Address:

Site / Account Name:

Website:

User Name:

eMail:

Membership / Rewards #:

Password: .... Date: ....

Password: .... Date: ....

Password: .... Date: ....

Password: .... Date: ....

Password: .... Date: ....

Password: .... Date: ....

Pin#:   Notes:

Secret Word:

Pass-phrase:

Phone# (associated with account):

Address:

Site / Account Name:

Website:

User Name:

eMail:

Membership / Rewards #:

Password: Date:

Password: Date:

Password: Date:

Password: Date:

Password: Date:

Password: Date:

Pin#: Notes:

Secret Word:

Pass-phrase:

Phone# (associated with account):

Address:

Site / Account Name:

Website:

User Name:

eMail:

Membership / Rewards #:

Password: Date:

Password: Date:

Password: Date:

Password: Date:

Password: Date:

Password: Date:

Pin#:   Notes:

Secret Word:

Pass-phrase:

Phone# (associated with account):

Address:

Site / Account Name:

Website:

User Name:

eMail:

Membership / Rewards #:

Password: Date:

Password: Date:

Password: Date:

Password: Date:

Password: Date:

Password: Date:

Pin#:   Notes:

Secret Word:

Pass-phrase:

Phone# (associated with account):

Address:

Site / Account Name:

Website:

User Name:

eMail:

Membership / Rewards #:

Password: Date:

Password: Date:

Password: Date:

Password: Date:

Password: Date:

Password: Date:

Pin#:   Notes:

Secret Word:

Pass-phrase:

Phone# (associated with account):

Address:

Site / Account Name:

Website:

User Name:

eMail:

Membership / Rewards #:

Password: .... Date:

Password: .... Date:

Password: .... Date:

Password: .... Date:

Password: .... Date:

Password: .... Date:

Pin#:   Notes:

Secret Word:

Pass-phrase:

Phone# (associated with account):

Address:

Site / Account Name:

Website:

User Name:

eMail:

Membership / Rewards #:

Password: .... Date:

Password: .... Date:

Password: .... Date:

Password: .... Date:

Password: .... Date:

Password: .... Date:

Pin#: .... Notes:

Secret Word:

Pass-phrase:

Phone# (associated with account):

Address:

Site / Account Name:

Website:

User Name:

eMail:

Membership / Rewards #:

Password: Date:

Password: Date:

Password: Date:

Password: Date:

Password: Date:

Password: Date:

Pin#: Notes:

Secret Word:

Pass-phrase:

Phone# (associated with account):

Address:

Site / Account Name:

Website:

User Name:

eMail:

Membership / Rewards #:

Password: Date:

Password: Date:

Password: Date:

Password: Date:

Password: Date:

Password: Date:

Pin#: Notes:

Secret Word:

Pass-phrase:

Phone# (associated with account):

Address:

Site / Account Name:

Website:

User Name:

eMail:

Membership / Rewards #:

Password: _____ Date: _____

Password: _____ Date: _____

Password: _____ Date: _____

Password: _____ Date: _____

Password: _____ Date: _____

Password: _____ Date: _____

Pin#: | Notes:

Secret Word:

Pass-phrase:

Phone# (associated with account):

Address:

Site / Account Name:

Website:

User Name:

eMail:

Membership / Rewards #:

Password: Date:

Password: Date:

Password: Date:

Password: Date:

Password: Date:

Password: Date:

Pin#:   Notes:

Secret Word:

Pass-phrase:

Phone# (associated with account):

Address:

Site / Account Name:

Website:

User Name:

eMail:

Membership / Rewards #:

Password: Date:

Password: Date:

Password: Date:

Password: Date:

Password: Date:

Password: Date:

Pin#:   Notes:

Secret Word:

Pass-phrase:

Phone# (associated with account):

Address:

Site / Account Name:

Website:

User Name:

eMail:

Membership / Rewards #:

Password: Date:

Password: Date:

Password: Date:

Password: Date:

Password: Date:

Password: Date:

Pin#:   Notes:

Secret Word:

Pass-phrase:

Phone# (associated with account):

Address:

Site / Account Name:

Website:

User Name:

eMail:

Membership / Rewards #:

Password: .... Date:

Password: .... Date:

Password: .... Date:

Password: .... Date:

Password: .... Date:

Password: .... Date:

Pin#: .... Notes:

Secret Word:

Pass-phrase:

Phone# (associated with account):

Address:

Site / Account Name:

Website:

User Name:

eMail:

Membership / Rewards #:

Password: Date:

Password: Date:

Password: Date:

Password: Date:

Password: Date:

Password: Date:

Pin#: Notes:

Secret Word:

Pass-phrase:

Phone# (associated with account):

Address:

Site / Account Name:

Website:

User Name:

eMail:

Membership / Rewards #:

Password: Date:

Password: Date:

Password: Date:

Password: Date:

Password: Date:

Password: Date:

Pin#: Notes:

Secret Word:

Pass-phrase:

Phone# (associated with account):

Address:

Site / Account Name:

Website:

User Name:

eMail:

Membership / Rewards #:

Password: Date:

Password: Date:

Password: Date:

Password: Date:

Password: Date:

Password: Date:

Pin#:   Notes:

Secret Word:

Pass-phrase:

Phone# (associated with account):

Address:

Site / Account Name:

Website:

User Name:

eMail:

Membership / Rewards #:

Password: Date:

Password: Date:

Password: Date:

Password: Date:

Password: Date:

Password: Date:

Pin#:   Notes:

Secret Word:

Pass-phrase:

Phone# (associated with account):

Address:

Site / Account Name:

Website:

User Name:

eMail:

Membership / Rewards #:

Password: .... Date:

Password: .... Date:

Password: .... Date:

Password: .... Date:

Password: .... Date:

Password: .... Date:

Pin#:   Notes:

Secret Word:

Pass-phrase:

Phone# (associated with account):

Address:

Site / Account Name:

Website:

User Name:

eMail:

Membership / Rewards #:

Password: Date:

Password: Date:

Password: Date:

Password: Date:

Password: Date:

Password: Date:

Pin#:   Notes:

Secret Word:

Pass-phrase:

Phone# (associated with account):

Address:

Site / Account Name:

Website:

User Name:

eMail:

Membership / Rewards #:

Password: Date:

Password: Date:

Password: Date:

Password: Date:

Password: Date:

Password: Date:

Pin#:   Notes:

Secret Word:

Pass-phrase:

Phone# (associated with account):

Address:

Site / Account Name:

Website:

User Name:

eMail:

Membership / Rewards #:

Password: Date:

Password: Date:

Password: Date:

Password: Date:

Password: Date:

Password: Date:

Pin#:   Notes:

Secret Word:

Pass-phrase:

Phone# (associated with account):

Address:

Site / Account Name:

Website:

User Name:

eMail:

Membership / Rewards #:

Password: Date:

Password: Date:

Password: Date:

Password: Date:

Password: Date:

Password: Date:

Pin#: Notes:

Secret Word:

Pass-phrase:

Phone# (associated with account):

Address:

Site / Account Name:

Website:

User Name:

eMail:

Membership / Rewards #:

Password: Date:

Password: Date:

Password: Date:

Password: Date:

Password: Date:

Password: Date:

Pin#: Notes:

Secret Word:

Pass-phrase:

Phone# (associated with account):

Address:

Site / Account Name:

Website:

User Name:

eMail:

Membership / Rewards #:

Password: Date:

Password: Date:

Password: Date:

Password: Date:

Password: Date:

Password: Date:

Pin#:   Notes:

Secret Word:

Pass-phrase:

Phone# (associated with account):

Address:

Site / Account Name:

Website:

User Name:

eMail:

Membership / Rewards #:

Password: Date:

Password: Date:

Password: Date:

Password: Date:

Password: Date:

Password: Date:

Pin#: Notes:

Secret Word:

Pass-phrase:

Phone# (associated with account):

Address:

Site / Account Name:

Website:

User Name:

eMail:

Membership / Rewards #:

Password: .... Date:

Password: .... Date:

Password: .... Date:

Password: .... Date:

Password: .... Date:

Password: .... Date:

Pin#: .... Notes:

Secret Word:

Pass-phrase:

Phone# (associated with account):

Address:

Site / Account Name:

Website:

User Name:

eMail:

Membership / Rewards #:

Password: Date:

Password: Date:

Password: Date:

Password: Date:

Password: Date:

Password: Date:

Pin#: Notes:

Secret Word:

Pass-phrase:

Phone# (associated with account):

Address:

Site / Account Name:

Website:

User Name:

eMail:

Membership / Rewards #:

Password: .... Date: ....

Password: .... Date: ....

Password: .... Date: ....

Password: .... Date: ....

Password: .... Date: ....

Password: .... Date: ....

Pin#: .... Notes:

Secret Word:

Pass-phrase:

Phone# (associated with account):

Address:

Site / Account Name:

Website:

User Name:

eMail:

Membership / Rewards #:

Password: Date:

Password: Date:

Password: Date:

Password: Date:

Password: Date:

Password: Date:

Pin#:   Notes:

Secret Word:

Pass-phrase:

Phone# (associated with account):

Address:

169

Site / Account Name:

Website:

User Name:

eMail:

Membership / Rewards #:

Password: Date:

Password: Date:

Password: Date:

Password: Date:

Password: Date:

Password: Date:

Pin#: Notes:

Secret Word:

Pass-phrase:

Phone# (associated with account):

Address:

Site / Account Name:

Website:

User Name:

eMail:

Membership / Rewards #:

Password: Date:

Password: Date:

Password: Date:

Password: Date:

Password: Date:

Password: Date:

Pin#:   Notes:

Secret Word:

Pass-phrase:

Phone# (associated with account):

Address:

Site / Account Name:

Website:

User Name:

eMail:

Membership / Rewards #:

Password: Date:

Password: Date:

Password: Date:

Password: Date:

Password: Date:

Password: Date:

Pin#:   Notes:

Secret Word:

Pass-phrase:

Phone# (associated with account):

Address:

Site / Account Name:

Website:

User Name:

eMail:

Membership / Rewards #:

Password: Date:

Password: Date:

Password: Date:

Password: Date:

Password: Date:

Password: Date:

Pin#:   Notes:

Secret Word:

Pass-phrase:

Phone# (associated with account):

Address:

173

Site / Account Name:

Website:

User Name:

eMail:

Membership / Rewards #:

Password: Date:

Password: Date:

Password: Date:

Password: Date:

Password: Date:

Password: Date:

Pin#: Notes:

Secret Word:

Pass-phrase:

Phone# (associated with account):

Address:

Site / Account Name:

Website:

User Name:

eMail:

Membership / Rewards #:

Password: Date:

Password: Date:

Password: Date:

Password: Date:

Password: Date:

Password: Date:

Pin#:   Notes:

Secret Word:

Pass-phrase:

Phone# (associated with account):

Address:

Site / Account Name:

Website:

User Name:

eMail:

Membership / Rewards #:

Password: Date:

Password: Date:

Password: Date:

Password: Date:

Password: Date:

Password: Date:

Pin#: Notes:

Secret Word:

Pass-phrase:

Phone# (associated with account):

Address:

Site / Account Name:

Website:

User Name:

eMail:

Membership / Rewards #:

Password: Date:

Password: Date:

Password: Date:

Password: Date:

Password: Date:

Password: Date:

Pin#:   Notes:

Secret Word:

Pass-phrase:

Phone# (associated with account):

Address:

Site / Account Name:

Website:

User Name:

eMail:

Membership / Rewards #:

Password: Date:

Password: Date:

Password: Date:

Password: Date:

Password: Date:

Password: Date:

Pin#:   Notes:

Secret Word:

Pass-phrase:

Phone# (associated with account):

Address:

Site / Account Name:

Website:

User Name:

eMail:

Membership / Rewards #:

Password: Date:

Password: Date:

Password: Date:

Password: Date:

Password: Date:

Password: Date:

Pin#: Notes:

Secret Word:

Pass-phrase:

Phone# (associated with account):

Address:

Site / Account Name:

Website:

User Name:

eMail:

Membership / Rewards #:

Password: Date:

Password: Date:

Password: Date:

Password: Date:

Password: Date:

Password: Date:

Pin#:   Notes:

Secret Word:

Pass-phrase:

Phone# (associated with account):

Address:

Site / Account Name:

Website:

User Name:

eMail:

Membership / Rewards #:

Password: Date:

Password: Date:

Password: Date:

Password: Date:

Password: Date:

Password: Date:

Pin#:   Notes:

Secret Word:

Pass-phrase:

Phone# (associated with account):

Address:

Site / Account Name:

Website:

User Name:

eMail:

Membership / Rewards #:

Password: Date:

Password: Date:

Password: Date:

Password: Date:

Password: Date:

Password: Date:

Pin#: Notes:

Secret Word:

Pass-phrase:

Phone# (associated with account):

Address:

Site / Account Name:

Website:

User Name:

eMail:

Membership / Rewards #:

Password: Date:

Password: Date:

Password: Date:

Password: Date:

Password: Date:

Password: Date:

Pin#:   Notes:

Secret Word:

Pass-phrase:

Phone# (associated with account):

Address:

183

Site / Account Name:

Website:

User Name:

eMail:

Membership / Rewards #:

Password: Date:

Password: Date:

Password: Date:

Password: Date:

Password: Date:

Password: Date:

Pin#:   Notes:

Secret Word:

Pass-phrase:

Phone# (associated with account):

Address:

Site / Account Name:

Website:

User Name:

eMail:

Membership / Rewards #:

Password: Date:

Password: Date:

Password: Date:

Password: Date:

Password: Date:

Password: Date:

Pin#:   Notes:

Secret Word:

Pass-phrase:

Phone# (associated with account):

Address:

Site / Account Name:

Website:

User Name:

eMail:

Membership / Rewards #:

Password: Date:

Password: Date:

Password: Date:

Password: Date:

Password: Date:

Password: Date:

Pin#:   Notes:

Secret Word:

Pass-phrase:

Phone# (associated with account):

Address:

Site / Account Name:

Website:

User Name:

eMail:

Membership / Rewards #:

Password: .... Date:

Password: .... Date:

Password: .... Date:

Password: .... Date:

Password: .... Date:

Password: .... Date:

Pin#:   Notes:

Secret Word:

Pass-phrase:

Phone# (associated with account):

Address:

187

Site / Account Name:

Website:

User Name:

eMail:

Membership / Rewards #:

Password: Date:

Password: Date:

Password: Date:

Password: Date:

Password: Date:

Password: Date:

Pin#: Notes:

Secret Word:

Pass-phrase:

Phone# (associated with account):

Address:

Site / Account Name:

Website:

User Name:

eMail:

Membership / Rewards #:

Password: Date:

Password: Date:

Password: Date:

Password: Date:

Password: Date:

Password: Date:

Pin#:   Notes:

Secret Word:

Pass-phrase:

Phone# (associated with account):

Address:

Site / Account Name:

Website:

User Name:

eMail:

Membership / Rewards #:

Password: _____ Date:

Password: _____ Date:

Password: _____ Date:

Password: _____ Date:

Password: _____ Date:

Password: _____ Date:

Pin#:   Notes:

Secret Word:

Pass-phrase:

Phone# (associated with account):

Address:

Site / Account Name:

Website:

User Name:

eMail:

Membership / Rewards #:

Password: Date:

Password: Date:

Password: Date:

Password: Date:

Password: Date:

Password: Date:

Pin#: Notes:

Secret Word:

Pass-phrase:

Phone# (associated with account):

Address:

Site / Account Name:

Website:

User Name:

eMail:

Membership / Rewards #:

Password: Date:

Password: Date:

Password: Date:

Password: Date:

Password: Date:

Password: Date:

Pin#:   Notes:

Secret Word:

Pass-phrase:

Phone# (associated with account):

Address:

Site / Account Name:

Website:

User Name:

eMail:

Membership / Rewards #:

Password: Date:

Password: Date:

Password: Date:

Password: Date:

Password: Date:

Password: Date:

Pin#:   Notes:

Secret Word:

Pass-phrase:

Phone# (associated with account):

Address:

Site / Account Name:

Website:

User Name:

eMail:

Membership / Rewards #:

Password: Date:

Password: Date:

Password: Date:

Password: Date:

Password: Date:

Password: Date:

Pin#:   Notes:

Secret Word:

Pass-phrase:

Phone# (associated with account):

Address:

Site / Account Name:

Website:

User Name:

eMail:

Membership / Rewards #:

Password: Date:

Password: Date:

Password: Date:

Password: Date:

Password: Date:

Password: Date:

Pin#:   Notes:

Secret Word:

Pass-phrase:

Phone# (associated with account):

Address:

195

Site / Account Name:

Website:

User Name:

eMail:

Membership / Rewards #:

Password: Date:

Password: Date:

Password: Date:

Password: Date:

Password: Date:

Password: Date:

Pin#:   Notes:

Secret Word:

Pass-phrase:

Phone# (associated with account):

Address:

Site / Account Name:

Website:

User Name:

eMail:

Membership / Rewards #:

Password: Date:

Password: Date:

Password: Date:

Password: Date:

Password: Date:

Password: Date:

Pin#:   Notes:

Secret Word:

Pass-phrase:

Phone# (associated with account):

Address:

Site / Account Name:

Website:

User Name:

eMail:

Membership / Rewards #:

Password: .... Date:

Password: .... Date:

Password: .... Date:

Password: .... Date:

Password: .... Date:

Password: .... Date:

Pin#: .... Notes:

Secret Word:

Pass-phrase:

Phone# (associated with account):

Address:

Site / Account Name:

Website:

User Name:

eMail:

Membership / Rewards #:

Password: Date:

Password: Date:

Password: Date:

Password: Date:

Password: Date:

Password: Date:

Pin#:   Notes:

Secret Word:

Pass-phrase:

Phone# (associated with account):

Address:

Site / Account Name:

Website:

User Name:

eMail:

Membership / Rewards #:

Password: Date:

Password: Date:

Password: Date:

Password: Date:

Password: Date:

Password: Date:

Pin#:   Notes:

Secret Word:

Pass-phrase:

Phone# (associated with account):

Address:

Site / Account Name:

Website:

User Name:

eMail:

Membership / Rewards #:

Password: Date:

Password: Date:

Password: Date:

Password: Date:

Password: Date:

Password: Date:

Pin#:   Notes:

Secret Word:

Pass-phrase:

Phone# (associated with account):

Address:

Site / Account Name:

Website:

User Name:

eMail:

Membership / Rewards #:

Password: .... Date:

Password: .... Date:

Password: .... Date:

Password: .... Date:

Password: .... Date:

Password: .... Date:

Pin#: .... Notes:

Secret Word:

Pass-phrase:

Phone# (associated with account):

Address:

Site / Account Name:

Website:

User Name:

eMail:

Membership / Rewards #:

Password: .... Date:

Password: .... Date:

Password: .... Date:

Password: .... Date:

Password: .... Date:

Password: .... Date:

Pin#:   Notes:

Secret Word:

Pass-phrase:

Phone# (associated with account):

Address:

Site / Account Name:

Website:

User Name:

eMail:

Membership / Rewards #:

Password: Date:

Password: Date:

Password: Date:

Password: Date:

Password: Date:

Password: Date:

Pin#:   Notes:

Secret Word:

Pass-phrase:

Phone# (associated with account):

Address:

Site / Account Name:

Website:

User Name:

eMail:

Membership / Rewards #:

Password: Date:

Password: Date:

Password: Date:

Password: Date:

Password: Date:

Password: Date:

Pin#: Notes:

Secret Word:

Pass-phrase:

Phone# (associated with account):

Address:

Site / Account Name:

Website:

User Name:

eMail:

Membership / Rewards #:

Password: Date:

Password: Date:

Password: Date:

Password: Date:

Password: Date:

Password: Date:

Pin#:   Notes:

Secret Word:

Pass-phrase:

Phone# (associated with account):

Address:

Site / Account Name:

Website:

User Name:

eMail:

Membership / Rewards #:

Password: Date:

Password: Date:

Password: Date:

Password: Date:

Password: Date:

Password: Date:

Pin#:   Notes:

Secret Word:

Pass-phrase:

Phone# (associated with account):

Address:

Site / Account Name:

Website:

User Name:

eMail:

Membership / Rewards #:

Password: Date:

Password: Date:

Password: Date:

Password: Date:

Password: Date:

Password: Date:

Pin#:   Notes:

Secret Word:

Pass-phrase:

Phone# (associated with account):

Address:

Site / Account Name:

Website:

User Name:

eMail:

Membership / Rewards #:

Password: Date:

Password: Date:

Password: Date:

Password: Date:

Password: Date:

Password: Date:

Pin#:   Notes:

Secret Word:

Pass-phrase:

Phone# (associated with account):

Address:

Site / Account Name:

Website:

User Name:

eMail:

Membership / Rewards #:

Password: Date:

Password: Date:

Password: Date:

Password: Date:

Password: Date:

Password: Date:

Pin#: Notes:

Secret Word:

Pass-phrase:

Phone# (associated with account):

Address:

Site / Account Name:

Website:

User Name:

eMail:

Membership / Rewards #:

Password: Date:

Password: Date:

Password: Date:

Password: Date:

Password: Date:

Password: Date:

Pin#:   Notes:

Secret Word:

Pass-phrase:

Phone# (associated with account):

Address:

Site / Account Name:

Website:

User Name:

eMail:

Membership / Rewards #:

Password: .... Date:

Password: .... Date:

Password: .... Date:

Password: .... Date:

Password: .... Date:

Password: .... Date:

Pin#: .... Notes:

Secret Word:

Pass-phrase:

Phone# (associated with account):

Address:

Site / Account Name:

Website:

User Name:

eMail:

Membership / Rewards #:

Password: Date:

Password: Date:

Password: Date:

Password: Date:

Password: Date:

Password: Date:

Pin#:   Notes:

Secret Word:

Pass-phrase:

Phone# (associated with account):

Address:

Site / Account Name:

Website:

User Name:

eMail:

Membership / Rewards #:

Password: .... Date:

Password: .... Date:

Password: .... Date:

Password: .... Date:

Password: .... Date:

Password: .... Date:

Pin#:

Secret Word:

Pass-phrase:

Phone# (associated with account):

Address:

Notes:

Site / Account Name:

Website:

User Name:

eMail:

Membership / Rewards #:

Password: .... Date:

Password: .... Date:

Password: .... Date:

Password: .... Date:

Password: .... Date:

Password: .... Date:

Pin#: .... Notes:

Secret Word:

Pass-phrase:

Phone# (associated with account):

Address:

Site / Account Name:

Website:

User Name:

eMail:

Membership / Rewards #:

Password: Date:

Password: Date:

Password: Date:

Password: Date:

Password: Date:

Password: Date:

Pin#: Notes:

Secret Word:

Pass-phrase:

Phone# (associated with account):

Address:

Site / Account Name:

Website:

User Name:

eMail:

Membership / Rewards #:

Password: Date:

Password: Date:

Password: Date:

Password: Date:

Password: Date:

Password: Date:

Pin#: Notes:

Secret Word:

Pass-phrase:

Phone# (associated with account):

Address:

Site / Account Name:

Website:

User Name:

eMail:

Membership / Rewards #:

Password: .... Date:

Password: .... Date:

Password: .... Date:

Password: .... Date:

Password: .... Date:

Password: .... Date:

Pin#:   Notes:

Secret Word:

Pass-phrase:

Phone# (associated with account):

Address:

Site / Account Name:

Website:

User Name:

eMail:

Membership / Rewards #:

Password: Date:

Password: Date:

Password: Date:

Password: Date:

Password: Date:

Password: Date:

Pin#:   Notes:

Secret Word:

Pass-phrase:

Phone# (associated with account):

Address:

Site / Account Name:

Website:

User Name:

eMail:

Membership / Rewards #:

Password: Date:

Password: Date:

Password: Date:

Password: Date:

Password: Date:

Password: Date:

Pin#:   Notes:

Secret Word:

Pass-phrase:

Phone# (associated with account):

Address:

Made in the USA
Columbia, SC
04 December 2019